EASY AS ABC

Ee

Warren Rylands and Katie Gillespie

LET'S READ
AV²
BY WEIGL™
ADDED VALUE • AUDIO VISUAL

Go to **www.av2books.com**, and enter this book's unique code.

BOOK CODE

R 5 9 6 2 9 3

AV² by Weigl brings you media enhanced books that support active learning.

AV² provides enriched content that supplements and complements this book. Weigl's AV² books strive to create inspired learning and engage young minds in a total learning experience.

Your AV² Media Enhanced books come alive with...

Audio
Listen to sections of the book read aloud.

Video
Watch informative video clips.

Embedded Weblinks
Gain additional information for research.

Try This!
Complete activities and hands-on experiments.

Key Words
Study vocabulary, and complete a matching word activity.

Quizzes
Test your knowledge.

Slide Show
View images and captions, and prepare a presentation.

... and much, much more!

Published by AV² by Weigl
350 5ᵗʰ Avenue, 59ᵗʰ Floor
New York, NY 10118

Website: www.av2books.com

Library of Congress Control Number: 2015940607

ISBN 978-1-4896-3483-2 (hardcover)
ISBN 978-1-4896-3485-6 (single user eBook)
ISBN 978-1-4896-3486-3 (multi-user eBook)

Printed in the United States of America in Brainerd, Minnesota
1 2 3 4 5 6 7 8 9 0 19 18 17 16 15

052015
WEP050815

Project Coordinator: Katie Gillespie   Art Director: Terry Paulhus

Weigl acknowledges Getty Images and iStock as the primary image suppliers for this title.

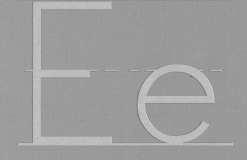

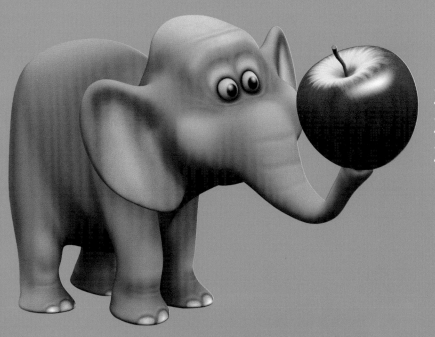

CONTENTS

Let's explore the letter

The uppercase letter **E** looks like this

The lowercase letter **e** looks like this

The letter  can start many words.

elephant

eye

exit

elk

eagle

7

The letter e can be inside a word.

bee

green

10

SEPTEMBER
7

tea

September

9

The letter e can be
at the end of a word.

stamped

bike

fire

doghouse

puzzle 11

Many names start with an uppercase E.

Emily

Erin can hop high.

Eduard is super cool.

Eric is strong.

Elizabeth loves ice cream.

The letter e makes different sounds.

zebra

jet

The word **zēbra** has a long ē sound.

The word **jĕt** has a short ĕ sound.

Some words have
a long ē sound.

ēach

mēans

ēat

rēad

sēa

Other words have
a short ĕ sound.

ĕnd

gĕt

sĕcond

lĕt

nĕxt

19

Having Fun with E

Eric the eagle lives in a tree.
In September, he reads by
the sea.

One day, Eric rode his bike
to the beach.

On his way to the sea, he saw
ten bees.
It was a stampede of bees.

Each bee wanted a second cup of tea.
Green tea is best for bees.

The alphabet has **26** letters.

E is the fifth letter in the alphabet.

Aa Bb Cc Dd **Ee**

Ff Gg Hh Ii Jj Kk

Ll Mm Nn Oo Pp

Qq Rr Ss Tt Uu Vv

Ww Xx Yy Zz

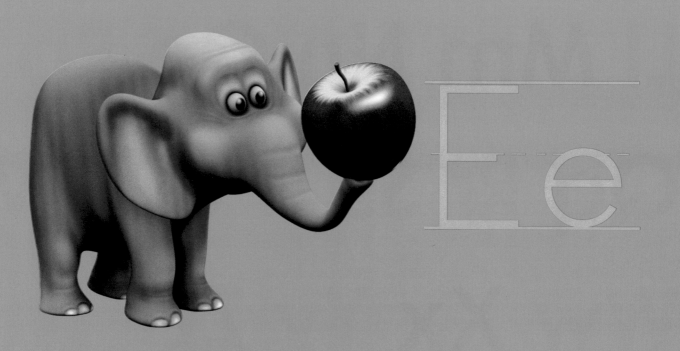